100

F

WHAT IS A CLASSIC?

WHAT IS A CLASSIC?

an address delivered before

the Virgil Society

on the

16th of October

1944

by

T. S. ELIOT

FABER & FABER LIMITED

24 Russell Square

London

First published in Mcmxlv
by Faber and Faber Limited
24 Russell Square London W.C. 1
Second Impression May Mcmxlv
Third Impression January Mcmxlvi
Printed in Great Britain by
R. MacLehose and Company Limited
The University Press Glasgow

WHAT IS A CLASSIC?

IN THE WHOLE OF EUROPEAN LITERATURE THERE IS
no poet who can furnish the texts for a more significant variety of discourse than Virgil. The fact that he
symbolises so much in the history of Europe, and represents such central European values, is the justification
for our founding a society to preserve his memory: the
fact that he is so central and so comprehensive is my
justification for this address. For if Virgil's poetry were a
subject upon which only scholars should presume to speak,
you would not have put me in this position, or have cared
to listen to what I have to say. I am emboldened by the reflection, that no specialised knowledge or proficiency can
confer the exclusive title to talk about Virgil. Speakers of
the most diverse capacities, can bring his poetry to bear
upon matters within their competence; can hope to con-
tribute, from those studies to which they have given their
minds, to the elucidation of his value; can try to offer, for
the general use, the benefit of whatever wisdom Virgil
may have helped them to acquire, in relation to their own
experience of life. Each can give his testimony of Virgil in
relation to those subjects which he knows best, or upon
which he has most deeply reflected: that is what I meant by
variety. In the end, we may all be saying the same thing in
different ways: and that is what I meant by significant
variety.

The subject which I have taken is simply the question:
'What is a classic?' It is not a new question. There is, for

instance, a famous essay by Ste. Beuve with this title: whether it is a misfortune or not, that—not having read it for some thirty-odd years—accidents of the present time have prevented me from re-reading it before preparing this address, I hope to find out as soon as libraries are more accessible and books more plentiful. The pertinence of asking this question, with Virgil particularly in mind, are obvious: whatever the definition we arrive at, it cannot be one which excludes Virgil—we may say confidently that it must be one which will expressly reckon with him. But before I go farther, I should like to dispose of certain prejudices and anticipate certain misunderstandings. I do not aim to supersede, or to outlaw, any use of the word 'classic' which precedent has made permissible. The word has, and will continue to have, several meanings in several contexts: I am concerned with one meaning in one context. In defining the term in this way, I do not bind myself, for the future, not to use the term in any of the other ways in which it has been used. If, for instance, you find me on some future occasion, in writing, in public speech, or in conversation, using the word 'classic' merely to mean a 'standard author' in any language—using it merely as an indication of the greatness, or of the permanence and importance of a writer in his own field, as when we speak of *The Fifth Form at St. Dominic's* as a classic of schoolboy fiction, or *Handley Cross* as a classic of the hunting field— you are not to expect an apology. And there is a very interesting book called *A Guide to the Classics*, which tells you how to pick the Derby winner. On other occasions, I permit myself to mean by 'the classics', either Latin and Greek literature *in toto*, or the greatest authors of those languages, as the context indicates. And, finally, I think that the account of the classic which I propose to give here

[8]

should remove it from the area of the antithesis between 'classic' and 'romantic'—a pair of terms belonging to literary politics, and therefore arousing passions which I should wish, on this occasion, Aeolus to contain in the bag.

This leads me to my next point. According to the terms of the classic-romantic controversy, the rules of that game, to call any work of art 'classical', implies either the highest praise or the most contemptuous abuse, according to the party to which one belongs. It implies certain particular merits or faults: either the perfection of form, or the absolute of frigidity. But I want to define one kind of art, and am not concerned that it is absolutely and in every respect *better* or *worse* than another kind. I shall enumerate certain qualities which I should expect the classic to display. But I do not say that, if a literature is to be a great literature, it must have any one author, or any one period, in which all these qualities are manifested. If, as I think, they are all to be found in Virgil, that is not to assert that he is the greatest poet who ever wrote—such an assertion about any poet seems to me meaningless—and it is certainly not to assert that Latin literature is greater than any other literature. We need not consider it as a defect of any literature, if no one author, or no one period, is completely classical; or if, as is true of English literature, the period which most nearly fills the classical definition is not the greatest. I think that those literatures, of which English is one of the most eminent, in which the classical qualities are scattered between various authors and several periods, may well be the richer. Every language has its own resources, and its own limitations. The conditions of a language, and the conditions of the history of the people who speak it, may put out of question the expectation of a classical period, or a classical author. That is not in itself any more a matter for regret than it is for gratulation. It did happen that the history of Rome was such, the character of the Latin language was such, that at a certain moment a uniquely classical poet was possible: though we must remember that it needed that particular poet, and a lifetime of labour on the part of that poet, to make the classic out of his material. And, of course, Virgil couldn't know that *that* was what he was doing. He was, if any poet ever was, acutely aware of what he was trying to do: the one thing he couldn't aim at, or know that he was doing, was to compose a classic: for it is only by hindsight, and in historical perspective, that a classic can be known as such.

If there is one word on which we can fix, which will suggest the maximum of what I mean by the term 'a classic', it is the word *maturity*. I shall distinguish between the universal classic, like Virgil, and the classic which is only such in relation to the other literature in its own language, or according to the view of life of a particular period. A classic can only occur when a civilisation is mature; when a language and a literature are mature; and it must be the work of a mature mind. It is the importance of that civilisation and of that language, as well as the comprehensiveness of the mind of the individual poet, which gives the universality. To define *maturity* without assuming that the hearer already knows what it means, is almost impossible: let us say then, that if we are properly mature, as well as educated persons, we can recognise maturity in a civilisation and in a literature, as we do in the other human beings whom we encounter. To make the meaning of maturity really apprehensible—indeed, even to make it acceptable—to the immature, is perhaps impossible. But if we are mature we either recognise maturity immediately, or come to know it on more intimate acquaintance.

[10]

No reader of Shakespeare, for instance, can fail to recognise, increasingly as he himself grows up, the gradual ripening of Shakespeare's mind: even a less developed reader can perceive the rapid development of Elizabethan literature and drama as a whole, from early Tudor crudity to the plays of Shakespeare, and perceive a decline in the work of Shakespeare's successors. We can also observe, upon a little conversance, that the plays of Christopher Marlowe exhibit a greater maturity of mind and of style, than the plays which Shakespeare wrote at the same age: it is interesting to speculate whether, if Marlowe had lived as long as Shakespeare, his development would have continued at the same pace. I doubt it: for we observe some minds maturing earlier than others, and we observe that those which mature very early do not always develop very far. I raise this point as a reminder, first that the value of maturity depends upon the value of that which matures, and second, that we should know when we are concerned with the maturity of individual writers, and when with the relative maturity of literary periods. A writer who individually has a more mature mind, may belong to a less mature period than another, so that in that respect his work will be less mature. The maturity of a literature is the reflection of that of the society in which it is produced: an individual author—notably Shakespeare and Virgil—can do much to develop his language: but he cannot bring that language to maturity unless the work of his predecessors has prepared it for his final touch. A mature literature, therefore, has a history behind it: a history, that is not merely a chronicle, an accumulation of manuscripts and writings of this kind and that, but an ordered though unconscious progress of a language to realise its own potentialities within its own limitations.

It is to be observed, that a society, and a literature, like an individual human being, do not necessarily mature equally and concurrently in every respect. The precocious child is often, in some obvious ways, childish for his age in comparison with ordinary children. Is there any one period of English literature to which we can point as being fully mature, comprehensively and in equilibrium? I do not think so: and, as I shall repeat later, I hope it is not so. We cannot say that any individual poet in English has in the course of his life become a more mature man than Shakespeare: we cannot even say that any poet has done so much, to make the English language capable of expressing the most subtle thought or the most refined shades of feeling. Yet we cannot but feel that a play like Congreve's *Way of the World* is in some way more mature than any play of Shakespeare's: but only in this respect, that it reflects a more mature society—that is, it reflects a greater maturity of *manners*. The society for which Congreve wrote was, from our point of view, coarse and brutal enough: yet it is nearer to ours than the society of the Tudors: perhaps for that reason we judge it the more severely. Nevertheless, it was a society more polished and less provincial: its mind was shallower, its sensibility more restricted; it has lost some promise of maturity but realised another. So to maturity of *mind* we must add maturity of *manners*.

The progress towards maturity of language is, I think, more easily recognised and more readily acknowledged in the development of prose, than in that of poetry. In considering prose we are less distracted by individual differences in greatness, and more inclined to demand approximation towards a common standard, a common vocabulary and a common sentence structure: it is often, in fact, the prose which departs the farthest from these common standards, which is individual to the extreme, that we are apt to denominate 'poetic prose'. At a time when England had already accomplished miracles in poetry, her prose was relatively immature, developed sufficiently for certain purposes but not for others: at that same time, when the French language had given little promise of poetry as great as that in English, French prose was much more mature than English prose. You have only to compare any Tudor writer with Montaigne—and Montaigne himself, as a stylist, is only a precursor, his style not ripe enough to fulfil the French requirements for the classic. Our prose was ready for some tasks before it could cope with others: a Malory could come long before a Hooker, a Hooker before a Hobbes, and a Hobbes before an Addison. Whatever difficulties we have in applying this standard to poetry, it is possible to see that the development of a classic prose is the development towards a *common style*. By this I do not mean that the best writers are indistinguishable from each other. The essential and characteristic differences remain: it is not that the differences are less, but that they are more subtle and refined. To a sensitive palate the difference between the prose of Addison and that of Swift will be as marked as the difference between two vintage wines to a connoisseur. What we find, in a period of classic prose, is not a mere common convention of writing, like the common style of newspaper leader writers, but a community of taste. The age which precedes a classic age, may exhibit both eccentricity and monotony: monotony, because the resources of the language have not yet been explored, and eccentricity because there is yet no generally accepted standard—if, indeed, that can be called eccentric where there is no centre. Its writing may be at the same time pedantic and licentious. The age following a classic age, may also exhibit eccentricity

[13]

and monotony: monotony because the resources of the language have, for the time at least, been exhausted, and eccentricity because originality comes to be more valued than correctness. But the age in which we find a common style, will be an age when society has achieved a moment of order and stability, of equilibrium and harmony; as the age which manifests the greatest extremes of individual style will be an age of development or an age of decay.

Maturity of language may naturally be expected to accompany maturity of mind and manners. We may expect the language to approach maturity at the moment when it has a critical sense of the past, a confidence in the present, and no conscious doubt of the future. In literature, this means that the poet is aware of his predecessors, and that we are aware of the predecessors behind his work, as we may be aware of ancestral traits in a person who is at the same time individual and unique. The predecessors should be themselves great and honoured: but their accomplishment must be such as to suggest still undeveloped resources of the language, and not such as to oppress the younger writers with the fear that everything that can be done has been done, in their language. The poet, certainly, in a mature age, may still obtain stimulus from the hope of doing something that his predecessors have not done; he may even be in revolt against them, as a promising adolescent may revolt against the beliefs, the habits and the manners of his parents; but, in retrospect, we can see that he is also the continuer of their traditions, that he preserves essential family characteristics, and that his difference of behaviour is a difference in the circumstances of another age. And, on the other hand, just as we sometimes observe men whose lives are overshadowed by the fame of a father or grandfather, men of whom any achievement of which they are capable appears comparatively insignificant, so a late age of poetry may be consciously impotent to compete with its distinguished paternity. We meet poets of this kind at the end of any age, poets with a sense of the past only, or alternatively, poets whose hope of the future is founded upon the attempt to renounce the past. The persistence of literary creativeness in any people, accordingly, consists in the maintenance of an unconscious balance between tradition in the larger sense—the collective personality, so to speak, realised in the literature of the past—and the originality of the living generation.

We cannot call the literature of the Elizabethan period, great as it is, wholly mature: we cannot call it classical. No close parallel can be drawn between the development of Greek and Latin literature, for Latin had Greek behind it; still less can we draw a parallel between these and any modern literature, for modern literatures had both Latin and Greek behind them. In the Renaissance there is an early semblance of maturity, which is borrowed from antiquity. We are aware of approaching nearer to maturity with Milton. Milton was in a better position to have a critical sense of the past—of a past in English literature—than his great predecessors. To read Milton is to be confirmed in respect for the genius of Spenser, and in gratitude to Spenser for having contributed towards making the verse of Milton possible. Yet the style of Milton is not a classic style: it is a style of a language still in formation, the style of a writer whose *masters* were not English, but Latin and to a less degree Greek. This, I think, is only saying what Johnson and in turn Landor said, when they complained of Milton's style not being quite English. Let us qualify this judgement by saying immediately that Milton did much to develop the language. One of the signs of approach towards a classic style is a development towards greater complexity of sentence and period structure. Such development is apparent in the single work of Shakespeare, when we trace his style from the early to the late plays: we can even say that in his late plays he goes as far in the direction of complexity as is possible within the limits of dramatic verse, which are narrower than those of other kinds. But complexity for its own sake is not a proper goal: its purpose must be, first, the precise expression of finer shades of feeling and thought; second, the introduction of greater refinement and variety of music. When an author appears, in his love of the elaborate structure, to have lost the ability to say anything simply; when his addiction to pattern becomes such that he says things elaborately which should properly be said simply, and thus limits his range of expression, the process of complexity ceases to be quite healthy, and the writer is losing touch with the spoken language. Nevertheless, as verse develops, in the hands of one poet after another, it tends from monotony to variety, from simplicity to complexity; as it declines, it tends towards monotony again, though it may perpetuate the formal structure to which genius gave life and meaning. You will judge for yourselves how far this generalisation is applicable to the predecessors and followers of Virgil: we can all see this secondary monotony in the eighteenth century imitators of Milton—who himself is never monotonous. There comes a time when a new simplicity, even a relative crudity, may be the only alternative.

You will have anticipated the conclusion towards which I have been approaching: that those qualities of the classic which I have so far mentioned—maturity of mind, maturity of manners, maturity of language and perfection of the common style—are most nearly to be illustrated, in English

[16]

literature, in the eighteenth century; and, in poetry, most in the poetry of Pope. If that were all I had to say on the matter, it would certainly not be new, and it would not be worth saying. That would be merely proposing a choice between two errors at which men have arrived before: one, that the eighteenth century is (as it thought itself) the finest period of English literature; and the other, that the classical idea should be wholly discredited. My own opinion is, that we have no classic age, and no classic poet, in English; that when we see why this is so, we have not the slightest reason for regret; but that, nevertheless, we must maintain the classic ideal before our eyes. Because we must maintain it, and because the English genius of language has had other things to do than to realise it, we cannot afford either to reject or to overrate the age of Pope; we cannot see English literature as a whole, or aim rightly in the future, without a critical appreciation of the degree to which the classical qualities are exemplified in the work of Pope: which means that unless we are able to enjoy the work of Pope, we cannot arrive at a full understanding of English poetry.

It is fairly obvious that the realisation of classical qualities by Pope was obtained at a high price—to the exclusion of some greater potentialities of English verse. Now, to some extent, the sacrifice of some potentialities in order to realise others, is a condition of artistic creation, as it is a condition of life in general. In life the man who refuses to sacrifice anything, to gain anything else, ends in mediocrity or failure; though, on the other hand, there is the specialist who has sacrificed too much for too little, or who has been born too completely the specialist to have had anything to sacrifice. But in the English eighteenth century, we have reason for feeling that too much was excluded. There was the mature mind: but it was a narrow one. English society and English letters were not provincial, in the sense that they were not isolated from, and not lingering behind, the best European society and letters. Yet the age itself was, in a manner of speaking, a provincial age. When one thinks of a Shakespeare, a Jeremy Taylor, a Milton, in England—of a Racine, a Molière, a Pascal, in France—in the seventeenth century, one is inclined to say that the eighteenth century had perfected its formal garden, only by restricting the area under cultivation. We feel that if the classic is really a worthy ideal, it must be capable of exhibiting an amplitude, a catholicity, to which the eighteenth century cannot lay claim; qualities which are present in some great authors, like Chaucer, who cannot be regarded in my sense as classics of English literature; and which are fully present in the mediaeval mind of Dante. For in the Divine Comedy, if anywhere, we find the classic in a modern European language. In the eighteenth century, we are oppressed by the limited range of sensibility, and especially in the scale of religious feeling. It is not that, in England at least, the poetry is not Christian. It is not even that the poets were not devout Christians: for a pattern of orthodoxy of principle, and sincere piety of feeling, you may look long before you find a poet more genuine than Samuel Johnson. Yet there are evidences of a deeper religious sensibility in the poetry of Shakespeare, whose belief and practice can be only a matter of conjecture. And this restriction of religious sensibility itself produces a kind of provinciality (though we must add that in this sense the nineteenth century was more provincial still): the provinciality which indicates the disintegration of Christendom, the decay of a common belief and a common culture. It would seem then, that the eighteenth century, in spite of its classical achievement—an achievement, I believe, which still has great importance as an example for the future—was lacking some condition which makes the creation of a true classic possible. What this condition is, we must return to Virgil to discover.

I should like first to rehearse the characteristics which I have already attributed to the classic, with special application to Virgil, to his language, his civilisation, and the particular moment in the history of that language and civilisation at which he arrived. Maturity of mind: this ✕ needs history, and the consciousness of history. Consciousness of history cannot be fully awake, except where there is other history than the history of the poet's own people: we need this in order to see our own place in history. There must be the knowledge of the history of at least one other highly civilised people, and of a people whose civilisation is sufficiently cognate to have influenced and entered into our own. This is a consciousness which the Romans had, and which the Greeks, however much more highly we may estimate their achievement—and indeed, we may respect it all the more on this account—could not possess. It was a consciousness, certainly, which Virgil himself did much to develop. From the beginning, Virgil, like his contemporaries and immediate predecessors, was constantly adapting and using the discoveries, traditions and inventions of Greek poetry: to make use of a foreign literature in this way marks a further stage of civilisation beyond making use only of the earlier stages of one's own—though I think we can say that no poet has ever shown a finer sense of proportion than Virgil, in the uses he made of Greek and of earlier Latin poetry. It is this development of one literature, or one civilisation, in relation to another, which gives a peculiar significance to the subject of Virgil's epic. In Homer, the conflict between the

[19]

Greeks and the Trojans is hardly larger in scope than a feud between one Greek city-state and a coalition of other city-states: behind the story of Aeneas is the consciousness of a more radical distinction, a distinction, which is at the same time a statement of *relatedness*, between two great cultures, and, finally, of their reconciliation under an all-embracing destiny.

Virgil's maturity of mind, and the maturity of his age, are exhibited in this awareness of history. With maturity of mind I have associated maturity of manners and absence of provinciality. I suppose that, to a modern European suddenly precipitated into the past, the social behaviour of the Romans and the Athenians would seem indifferently coarse, barbarous and offensive. But if the poet can portray something superior to contemporary practice, it is not in the way of anticipating some later, and quite different code of behaviour, but by an insight into what the conduct of his own people at his own time might be, at its best. House parties of the wealthy, in Edwardian England, were not exactly what we read of in the pages of Henry James: but Mr. James's society was an idealisation, of a kind, of *that* society, and not an anticipation of any other. I think that we are conscious, in Virgil more than in any other Latin poet—for Catullus and Propertius seem ruffians, and Horace somewhat plebeian, by comparison—of a refinement of manners springing from a delicate sensibility, and particularly in that test of manners, private and public conduct between the sexes. It is not for me, in a gathering of people, all of whom may be better scholars than I, to review the story of Aeneas and Dido. But I have always thought the meeting of Aeneas with the shade of Dido, in Book VI, not only one of the most poignant, but one of the most civilised passages in poetry. It is complex in meaning and economical in expression, for it not only tells us about the attitude of Dido—what is still more important is what it tells us about the attitude of Aeneas. Dido's behaviour appears almost as a projection of Aeneas' own conscience: this, we feel, is the way in which Aeneas' conscience would *expect* Dido to behave to him. The point, it seems to me, is not that Dido is unforgiving—though it is important that, instead of railing at him, she merely snubs him—perhaps the most telling snub in all poetry: what matters most is, that Aeneas does not forgive himself—and this, significantly, in spite of the fact of which he is well aware, that all that he has done has been in compliance with destiny, or in consequence of the machinations of gods who are themselves, we feel, only instruments of a greater inscrutable power. Here, what I chose as an instance of civilised manners, proceeds to testify to civilised consciousness and conscience: but all of the levels at which we may consider a particular episode, belong to one whole. It will be observed, finally, that the behaviour of Virgil's characters (I might except Turnus, the man without a destiny) never appears to be according to some purely local or tribal code of manners: it is, in its time, both Roman and European. Virgil certainly, on the plane of manners, is not provincial.

To attempt to demonstrate the maturity of language and style of Virgil is, for the present occasion, a superfluous task: many of you could perform it better than I, and I think that we should all be in accord. But it is worth repeating that Virgil's style would not have been possible without a literature behind him, and without his having a very intimate knowledge of this literature: so that he was, in a sense, re-writing Latin poetry—as when he borrows a phrase or a device from a predecessor and improves upon it. He was a learned author, all of whose learning was relevant to his task; and he had, for his use, just enough literature behind him and not too much. As for maturity of style, I do not think that any poet has ever developed a greater command of the complex structure, both of sense and sound, without losing the resource of direct, brief and startling simplicity when the occasion required it. On this I need not dilate: but I think it is worth while to say a word more about the *common style*, because this is something which we cannot perfectly illustrate from English poetry, and we are therefore apt to pay not enough deference to it. In modern European literature, the closest approximation to the ideal of a common style, is probably to be found in Dante and in Racine; the nearest we have to it in English poetry is Pope, and Pope's is a common style which, in comparison, is of a very narrow range. A common style is one which makes us exclaim, not 'this is a man of genius using the language' but 'this realises the genius of the language'. We do not say this when we read Pope, because we are too conscious of all the resources of the English speech upon which Pope does not draw; we can at most say 'this realises the genius of the English language of a particular epoch'. We do not say this when we read Shakespeare or Milton, because we are always conscious of the greatness of the man, and of the miracles that *he* is performing with the language; we come nearer perhaps with Chaucer—but that Chaucer is using a different, from our point of view a cruder speech. And Shakespeare and Milton, as later history shows, left open many possibilities of other uses of English in poetry: whereas, after Virgil, it is truer to say that no great development was possible, until the Latin language became something different.

At this point I should like to return to a question which I have already suggested: the question whether the achievement of a classic, in the sense in which I have been using the term throughout, is, for the people and the language of its origin, altogether an unmixed blessing—even though it is unquestionably a ground for pride. To have this question raised in one's mind, it is almost enough simply to have contemplated Latin poetry after Virgil, to have considered the extent to which later poets lived and worked under the shadow of his greatness: so that we praise or dispraise them, according to standards which he set—admiring them, sometimes, for discovering some variation which was new, or even for merely rearranging patterns of words so as to give a pleasing faint reminder of the remote original. We may raise a rather different question, when we view Italian poetry after Dante: for the later Italian poets did not imitate Dante, and had this advantage, that they lived in a world which was more rapidly changing, so that there was obviously something different for them to do; they provoke no direct disastrous comparison. But English poetry, and French poetry also, may be considered fortunate in this: that the greatest poets have exhausted only particular areas. We cannot say that, since the age of Shakespeare, and respectively since the time of Racine, there has been any really first-rate poetic drama in England or in France; since Milton, we have had no great epic poem, though there have been great long poems. It is true that every supreme poet, classic or not, tends to exhaust the ground he cultivates, so that it must, after yielding a diminishing crop, finally be left in fallow for some generations.

Here you may object that the effect on a literature which I am imputing to the classic, results not from the classic character of that work, but simply from its greatness: for I have denied to Shakespeare and to Milton the title of classics, in the sense in which I am employing the term throughout, and yet have admitted that no supremely great poetry of the same kind has been written since. You may or may not be disposed to accept the distinction which I shall make. That every great work of poetry tends to make impossible the production of equally great works of the same kind is indisputable. The reason may be stated partly in terms of conscious purpose: no first-rate poet would attempt to do again, what has already been done as well as it can be done in his language. It is only after the language —its cadence, still more than vocabulary and syntax—has, with time and social change, sufficiently altered, that another dramatic poet as great as Shakespeare, or another epic poet as great as Milton, can become possible. Not only every great poet, but every genuine, though lesser poet, fulfils once for all some possibility of the language, and so leaves one possibility less for his successors. The vein that he has exhausted may be a very small one; or may represent some major form of poetry, the epic or dramatic. But what the great poet has exhausted is merely one form, and not the whole language. The classic poet, on the other hand, exhausts, not a form only, but the language of his time; and when he is a wholly classic poet, the language of his time will be the language in its perfection. So that it is not the poet alone of whom we have to take account, but the language in which he writes: it is not merely that a classic poet exhausts the language, but that an exhaustible language is the kind which may produce a classic poet.

We may be inclined to ask, then, whether we are not fortunate in possessing a language which, instead of having produced a classic, can boast a rich variety in the past, and the possibility of further novelty in the future? Now while we are *inside* a literature, while we speak the same language, and have fundamentally the same culture as that which produced the literature of the past, we want to maintain two things: a pride in what our literature has already accomplished, and a belief in what it may still accomplish in the future. If we cease to believe in the future, the past would cease to be fully *our* past: it would become the past of a dead civilisation. And this consideration must operate with particular cogency upon the minds of those who are engaged in the attempt to add to the store of English literature. There is no classic in English: therefore, any living poet can say, there is still hope that I—and those after me, for no one can face with equanimity, once he understands what is implied, the thought of being the *last* poet—may be able to write something which will be worth preserving. But from the aspect of eternity, such interest in the future has no meaning: when two languages are both dead languages, we cannot say that one is greater, because of the number and variety of its poets, or the other because its genius is more completely expressed in the work of one poet. What I wish to affirm, at one and the same time, is this: that, because English is a living language and the language in which we live, we may be glad that it has never completely realised itself in the work of one classic poet; but that, on the other hand, the classic criterion is of vital importance to us. We need it in order to judge our individual poets, though we refuse to judge our literature as a whole in comparison with one which has produced a classic. Whether a literature does culminate in a classic, is a matter of fortune. It is largely, I suspect, a question of the degree of fusion of the elements within that language; so that the Latin languages can approximate more closely to the classic, not simply because they are Latin, but because they are more homogeneous than English, and therefore tend more naturally towards the *common style*: whereas English, being the most various of great languages in its constituents, tends to variety rather than perfection, needs the longest time to realise its potency, and still contains, perhaps, more unexplored possibilities. It has, perhaps, the greatest capacity for changing, and yet remaining itself.

I am now approaching the distinction between the relative and the absolute classic, the distinction between the literature which can be called classic in relation to its own language, and that which is classic in relation to a number of other languages. But first I wish to record one more characteristic of the classic, beyond those I have enumerated, which will help to establish this distinction, and to mark the difference between such a classic as Pope and such a classic as Virgil. It is convenient to recapitulate certain assertions which I made earlier.

I suggested, at the beginning, that a frequent, if not universal feature of the maturing of individuals may be a process of selection (not altogether conscious), of the development of some potentialities to the exclusion of others; and that a similarity may be found in the development of language and literature. If this is so, we should expect to find that in a minor classic literature, such as our own of the late seventeenth and the eighteenth century, the elements excluded, to arrive at maturity, will be more numerous or more serious; and that satisfaction in the result, will always be qualified by our awareness of the possibilities of the language, revealed in the work of earlier authors, which have been ignored. The classic age of English literature is not representative of the total genius of the race: as I have intimated, we cannot say that that genius is wholly realised in any one period—with the result that we can still, by referring to one or another period of the past, envisage possibilities for the future. The English language is one which offers wide scope for legitimate divergencies of style; it seems to be such that no one age, and certainly no one writer, can establish a norm. The French language has seemed to be much more closely tethered to a normal style; yet, even in French, though the language appeared to have established itself, once for all, in the seventeenth century, there is an *esprit gaulois*, an element of richness present in Rabelais and in Villon, the awareness of which may qualify our judgement of the *wholeness* of Racine or Molière, for we may feel that it is not only unrepresented but unreconciled. We may come to the conclusion, then, that the perfect classic must be one in which the whole genius of a people will be latent, if not all revealed; and that it can only appear in a language such that its whole genius can be present at once. We must accordingly add, to our list of characteristics of the classic, that of *comprehensiveness*. The classic must, within its formal limitations, express the maximum possible of the whole range of feeling which represents the character of the people who speak that language. It will represent this at its best, and it will also have the widest appeal: among the people to which it belongs, it will find its response among all classes and conditions of men.

When a work of literature has, beyond this comprehensiveness in relation to its own language, an equal significance in relation to a number of foreign literatures, we may say that it has also *universality*. We may for instance speak justly enough of the poetry of Goethe as constituting a classic, because of the place which it occupies in its own language and literature. Yet, because of its partiality, of the impermanence of some of its content, and the germanism of the sensibility; because Goethe appears, to a foreign eye, limited by his age, by his language, and by his culture, so that he is unrepresentative of the whole European tradition, and, like our own nineteenth century authors, a little provincial, we cannot call him a *universal* classic. He is a universal author, in the sense that he is an author with whose works every European ought to be acquainted: but that is a different thing. Nor, on one count or another, can we expect to find the proximate approach to the classic in *any* modern language. It is necessary to go to the two dead languages: it is important that they are dead, because through their death we have come into our inheritance—the fact that they are dead would in itself give them no value, apart from the fact that all the peoples of Europe are their beneficiaries. And of all the great poets of Greece and Rome, I think that it is to Virgil that we owe the most for our standard of the classic: which, I will repeat, is not the same thing as pretending that he is the greatest, or the one to whom we are in every way the most indebted—it is of a particular debt that I speak. His comprehensiveness, his peculiar kind of comprehensiveness, is due to the unique position in our history of the Roman Empire and the Latin language: a position which may be said to conform to its *destiny*. This sense of destiny comes to consciousness in the Aeneid. Aeneas is himself, from first to last, a 'man in fate', a man who is neither an adventurer nor a schemer, neither a vagabond nor a careerist, a man fulfilling his destiny, not under compulsion or arbitrary decree, and certainly from no stimulus to glory, but by surrendering his will to a higher power behind the gods who would thwart or direct him. He would have preferred to stop in Troy, but he becomes an exile, and something greater and more significant than any exile; he is exiled for a purpose greater than he can know, but which he recognises; and he is not, in a human sense, a happy or successful man. But he is the symbol

[28]

of Rome; and, as Aeneas is to Rome, so is ancient Rome to Europe. Thus Virgil acquires the centrality of the unique classic; he is at the centre of European civilisation, in a position which no other poet can share or usurp. The Roman Empire and the Latin language were not any empire and any language, but an empire and a language with a unique destiny in relation to ourselves; and the poet in whom that Empire and that language came to consciousness and expression is a poet of unique destiny.

If Virgil is thus the consciousness of Rome and the supreme voice of her language, he must have a significance for us which cannot be expressed wholly in terms of literary appreciation and criticism. Yet, adhering to the problems of literature, or to the terms of literature in dealing with life, we may be allowed to imply more than we state. The value of Virgil to us, in literary terms, is in providing us with a critical criterion. We may, as I have said, have reasons to rejoice that this criterion is provided by a poet writing in a different language from our own: but that is not a reason for rejecting the criterion. To preserve the classical standard, and to measure every individual work of literature by it, is to see that, while our literature as a whole may contain everything, every single work in it may be defective in something. This may be a necessary defect, a defect without which some quality present would be lacking: but we must see it as a defect, at the same time that we see it as a necessity. In the absence of this standard of which I speak, a standard we cannot keep clearly before us if we rely on our own literature alone, we tend, first to admire works of genius for the wrong reasons —as we extol Blake for his *philosophy*, and Hopkins for his *style*: and from this we proceed to greater error, to giving the second-rate equal rank with the first-rate. In short, without the constant application of the classical measure, which we owe to Virgil more than to any other one poet, we tend to become provincial.

By 'provincial' I mean here something more than I find in the dictionary definitions. I mean more, for instance, than 'wanting the culture or polish of the capital', though, certainly, Virgil was of the Capital, to a degree which makes any later poet of equal stature look a little provincial; and I mean more than 'narrow in thought, in culture, in creed'—a slippery definition this, for, from a modern liberal point of view, Dante was 'narrow in thought, in culture, in creed', yet it may be the Broad Churchman, rather than the Narrow Churchman, who is the more provincial. I mean also a distortion of values, the exclusion of some, the exaggeration of others, which springs, not from lack of wide geographical perambulation, but from applying standards acquired within a limited area, to the whole of human experience; which confounds the contingent with the essential, the ephemeral with the permanent. In our age, when men seem more than ever prone to confuse wisdom with knowledge, and knowledge with information, and to try to solve problems of life, in terms of engineering, there is coming into existence a new kind of provincialism which perhaps deserves a new name. It is a provincialism, not of space, but of time; one for which history is merely the chronicle of human devices which have served their turn and been scrapped, one for which the world is the property solely of the living, a property in which the dead hold no shares. The menace of this kind of provincialism is, that we can all, all the peoples on the globe, be provincials together; and those who are not content to be provincials, can only become hermits. If this kind of provincialism led to greater tolerance, in the sense of forbearance, there might be more to be said for it; but it seems more likely to lead to our becoming indifferent, in matters where we ought to maintain a distinctive dogma or standard, and to our becoming intolerant, in matters which might be left to local or personal preference. We may have as many varieties of religion as we like, provided we all send our children to the same schools. But my concern here is only with the corrective to provincialism in literature. We need to remind ourselves that, as Europe is a whole (and still, in its progressive mutilation and disfigurement, the organism out of which any greater world harmony must develop), so European literature is a whole, the several members of which cannot flourish, if the same blood-stream does not circulate throughout the whole body. The blood-stream of European literature is Latin and Greek—not as two systems of circulation, but one, for it is through Rome that our parentage in Greece must be traced. What common measure of excellence have we in literature, among our several languages, which is not the classical measure? What mutual intelligibility can we hope to preserve, except in our common heritage of thought and feeling in those two languages, for the understanding of which, no European people is in any position of advantage over any other? No modern language could aspire to the universality of Latin, even though it came to be spoken by millions more than ever spoke Latin, and even though it came to be the universal means of communication between peoples of all tongues and cultures. No modern language can hope to produce a classic, in the sense in which I have called Virgil a classic. Our classic, the classic of all Europe, is Virgil.

In our several literatures, we have much wealth of which to boast, to which Latin has nothing to compare; but each literature has its greatness, not in isolation, but because of its place in a larger pattern, a pattern set in Rome. I have spoken of the new seriousness—*gravity* I might say—the new insight into history, illustrated by the dedication of Aeneas to Rome, to a future far beyond his living achievement. *His* reward was hardly more than a narrow beachhead and a political marriage in a weary middle age: his youth interred, its shadow moving with the shades the other side of Cumae. And so, I said, one envisages the destiny of ancient Rome. So we may think of Roman literature: at first sight, a literature of limited scope, with a poor muster of great names, yet universal as no other literature can be; a literature unconsciously sacrificing, in compliance to its destiny in Europe, the opulence and variety of later tongues, to produce, for us, the classic. It is sufficient that this standard should have been established once for all: the task does not have to be done again. But the maintenance of the standard is the price of our freedom, the defence of freedom against chaos. We may remind ourselves of this obligation, by our annual observance of piety towards the great ghost who guided Dante's pilgrimage: who, as it was his function to lead Dante towards a vision he could never himself enjoy, led Europe towards the Christian culture which he could never know; and who, speaking for the last time in the new Italian speech, said in farewell

il temporal foco e l'eterno
veduto hai, figlio, e sei venuto in parte
dov' io per me più oltre non discerno.

Son, the temporal fire and the eternal, hast
thou seen, and art come to a place where I,
of myself, discern no further.

[32]